SCHOOL LIBRARIES

THE SECRET WORLD OF

Bats

THE SECRET WORLD OF Bats

Theresa Greenaway

www.raintreepublishers.co.uk
Visit our website to find out more information about **Raintree** books.

To order:
 Phone 44 (0) 1865 888112
 Send a fax to 44 (0) 1865 314091
 Visit the Raintree Bookshop at www.raintreepublishers.co.uk to browse our catalogue and order online.

First published in Great Britain by Raintree,
Halley Court, Jordan Hill, Oxford
OX2 8EJ, part of Harcourt Education.
Raintree is a registered trademark of Harcourt Education Ltd.

Produced for Raintree by Discovery Books
Editors: Kathryn Walker and Catherine Clarke
Consultant: Michael Chinery
Design: Ian Winton
Illustrations: Stuart Lafford, Colin Newman, Keith Williams
Production: Jonathan Smith

Originated by Dot Gradations Ltd
Printed and bound in China by South China Printing Company

ISBN 1 844 21584 9 (hardback)
07 06 05 04 03
10 9 8 7 6 5 4 3 2 1

British Library Cataloguing in Publication Data
Greenaway, Theresa,
The Secret World of Bats
599.4
A full catalogue record for this book is available from the British Library.

Acknowledgements
The publishers would like to thank the following for permission to reproduce photographs:
Bruce Coleman Collection pp. **12**, **21** (Kim Taylor), **25** (Jane Burton), **30** bottom (Jens Rydell), **31** (M.P.L. Fogden); Natural History Photographic Agency pp. **9** bottom (Melvin Grey), **11** (Daniel Heuclin), **14** top (Daniel Heuclin), **17** and **19** (Stephen Dalton), **22** (Ken Griffiths), **23** top (A.N.T. Photo Library), **24** (Stephen Dalton), **26** top and bottom: (Stephen Dalton), **27** (Haroldo Palo Jr.), **28** (Anthony Bannister), **29** top (Eric Soder), **29** bottom (Ann and Steve Toon), **32** and **33** (Melvin Grey), **34** (A.N.T.), **36** (Kevin Schafer), **37** (Daniel Heuclin), **38** (Roger Tidman), **39** (Stephen Krasemann), **40** (Brian Hawkes), **41** (Stephen Krasemann), **42** (David Woodfall), **43** (Nick Garbutt); Oxford Scientific Films pp. **8** (H. and J. Beste), **9** top (Wendy Shattil and Bob Rozinski), **10** (Babs and Bert Wells), **14** bottom (Stephen Dalton), **15** top (Paul Franklin), **15** bottom (Presstige Pictures), **20** (John Mitchell), **23** bottom (Michael Pitts), **30** top (Richard Packwood).
All background images © Steck-Vaughn Collection (Corbis Royalty Free, Getty Royalty Free, and StockBYTE).
Cover photograph reproduced with permission of the Bruce Coleman Collection.

Every effort has been made to contact copyright holders of any material reproduced in this book. Any omissions will be rectified in subsequent printings if notice is given to the publishers.

Any words appearing in the text in bold, like this, are explained in the Glossary.

Contents

Mammals that fly

The largest of all bats are the Indian flying fox, the Indonesian fruit bat and the golden-capped fruit bat, which is found in the Philippines. These megabats have wingspans of about 1.7 metres and weigh 1.5 kilograms or more.

The smallest megabat is the flower bat from Malaysia, which has a wingspan of 21–24 centimetres.

The largest microbat is the false vampire bat that lives in the American tropics, with a wingspan of almost 1 metre.

The smallest microbat is the bumblebee bat, also known as Kitti's hog-nosed bat. It lives in Thailand and is possibly the smallest mammal in the world, weighing just 1.5 grams.

Bats are **mammals**, just like cats, horses and humans. They have fur, they feed their young with milk from the mother's body and they are warm-blooded **endotherms**. This means that they can generate and maintain their own body heat.

All bats belong to the order, or group, of mammals called the **Chiroptera**. 'Chiroptera' means 'hand wing': the bat's fingers, connected by a stretchy **membrane**, make up most of each wing. There are about 957 **species** of Chiroptera, and these are divided into two groups:
• megabats, or fruit bats
• microbats, also known as insect-eating bats, although they do not all eat insects.
In fact, many microbats also eat fruit. Not all megabats are large – some of them are much smaller than the largest microbats.

Bats are the only mammals that can fly. Many mammals can glide, supported by a wide band of skin tightly stretched between their front and rear **limbs**, but bats actually flap their wings using powerful muscles.

Bats are **nocturnal**, which means they move about and hunt at night.

To help them find their way and their **prey**, microbats send out high-pitched sounds and listen for the echoes made by the sound waves bouncing off nearby objects. This is called **echolocation**.

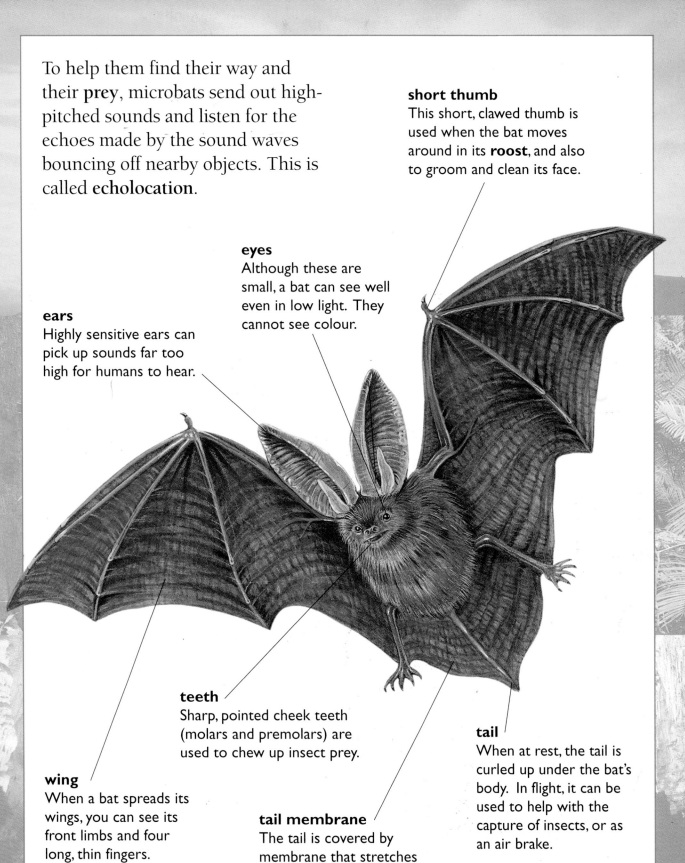

short thumb
This short, clawed thumb is used when the bat moves around in its **roost**, and also to groom and clean its face.

eyes
Although these are small, a bat can see well even in low light. They cannot see colour.

ears
Highly sensitive ears can pick up sounds far too high for humans to hear.

teeth
Sharp, pointed cheek teeth (molars and premolars) are used to chew up insect prey.

wing
When a bat spreads its wings, you can see its front limbs and four long, thin fingers.

tail membrane
The tail is covered by membrane that stretches between the two back legs.

tail
When at rest, the tail is curled up under the bat's body. In flight, it can be used to help with the capture of insects, or as an air brake.

MEGABATS

There are about 175 **species** of megabat. These all live in the warm **tropical** and **subtropical** parts of Africa, Asia and Australia. Because they have long muzzles and large eyes, giving them a fox-like appearance, megabats are often called 'flying foxes'. They are also sometimes known as the 'Old World' fruit bats, to tell them apart from American fruit-eating bats, which are in fact microbats.

When resting, a megabat holds its head at a right angle to the line of its body. It has large eyes, molar teeth that are usually smooth, with no **cusps** or points, and usually two claws on each wing. Megabats have either small tails, or no tails at all. Most megabats **navigate** by sight.

This black flying fox has the large eyes and fox-like face common to megabats. It is looking straight ahead, with its head at a right angle to its body.

A microbat's front teeth (incisors) are usually so tiny that they cannot be seen without magnification, but the cheek teeth, like those of this little brown bat, can clearly be seen.

MICROBATS

There are about 782 species of microbat. When resting, a microbat holds its head in line with its body. It has small eyes, sharply cusped molar teeth and only one claw on each wing. Microbats have tails, which in a few species may be quite long. They also have highly developed **echolocation** systems.

Microbats are found on all continents except Antarctica. Those that live in places with cold winters **hibernate** during the coldest weather. In summer, North America's little brown bat is one of a few **species** that live just north of the Arctic Circle, although it **migrates** south in winter. At least two species, the South American big-eared brown bat and *Myotis chiloensis*, are found as far south as Tierra del Fuego in South America.

The noctule is a common insect-eating microbat. It has large ears and small eyes. The pink area on the shoulder of this bat is not a wound – it is a scent **gland**.

9

BATS EVERYWHERE

Bats live in all sorts of **habitats**. There are desert bats, bats of woodlands and tropical rainforests, and those that live in towns and cities. Many even make their homes inside houses. There are more kinds of bats found in the **tropical** regions of the world than in the cooler regions.

COLOUR

Most bats range in colour from the blackish brown of the European barbastelle to the reddish brown of the North American red bat. Among the most brightly coloured are the painted bats of south-east Asia and Africa, which have reddish-orange fur and black wings. Some **species** have patterns of white spots, such as the American spotted bat, or white lines or stripes and patches, such as the African butterfly bat. The

It is easy to see how this ghost bat from Australia got its name. With its almost white wings and pale, silvery-grey fur, it looks like a ghost flitting by in the night.

ghost bat is almost white, while the bulldog bat, which lives in Malaysia, the Philippines and Borneo, has almost no fur at all.

Funny faces

Some species, such as the horseshoe, slit-faced and spear-nosed (shown here) bats, have parts of all shapes and sizes sticking out from their faces, making them look quite funny. Many of these flaps and folds of skin are thought to help focus the sounds the bat makes during **echolocation**. Perhaps the strangest face belongs to the wrinkle-faced bat from Central America, whose face is a mass of folds. When hanging upside down, its face is hidden by a transparent chin flap that it can see through!

On the move

The short-tailed bat from New Zealand spends much more time on the ground than other bats. It hunts for insects in the burrows of ground-nesting birds.

Fisherman bats, from South and Central America, are good swimmers and can take off from the surface of the water.

A bat's body has to be light enough for its wings to keep it airborne, so bats have thin bones.

The long-tongued bat darts from flower to flower, hovering in front of each, like a hummingbird.

Many bats can fly at speeds of up to 48 kilometres (30 miles) per hour, but the fastest recorded so far is 64 kilometres (40 miles) per hour, achieved by the American big brown bat.

A bat's main way of moving about is flying. The ability to fly gives bats many advantages. It means they are able to search for food over a wide area, which gives them much more choice of food sources. They can travel long distances to search for good **roost** sites in which to mate, **hibernate** or sleep. Flight gives bats a way of escaping from **predators** that cannot fly.

A BAT'S WING

A bat's wing is like a hand with very long fingers connected by a thin, elastic **membrane**. This membrane extends along the sides of its body and down the legs, leaving the clawed feet free. Many kinds of bats also have a tail

Bats, like this short-tailed bat, can flex their wings by moving their fingers and their legs. This means they can change direction quickly.

membrane that is connected to both legs. The membranes are made of an upper and lower layer of hairless skin and contain thin muscles and elastic fibres. These help to keep the wings stiff during flight and also allow the bat to fold its wings away when not in use. Flight is powered by strong muscles in the chest and back. Bats can change direction by flexing one or more 'fingers', giving them great **agility** in the air.

How wings work

A bat does not just flap its wings up and down, but twists and turns them in a figure-of-eight pattern. On the downstroke, the wings are fully extended, pushing the bat forward and keeping the air flowing over them. During the upstroke, the wings are bent slightly to reduce **air resistance**.

Different kinds of bats fly in different ways. Horseshoe bats, leaf-nosed bats and others that search for food among the leafy branches of trees fly slowly or hover and have quite short, broad wings. **Species** that fly swiftly in order to hunt insects, such as the moustached bat, have long, narrow wings.

How wings work

Wings work because their upper surface is convex, or curved outwards, and therefore longer than their lower surface. Air flowing over the top of the wing moves faster and so puts less **pressure** on the wing.

The greater pressure on the lower surface of the wing gives it lift. The wings keep a constant stream of air flowing over them, so the bat stays in the air.

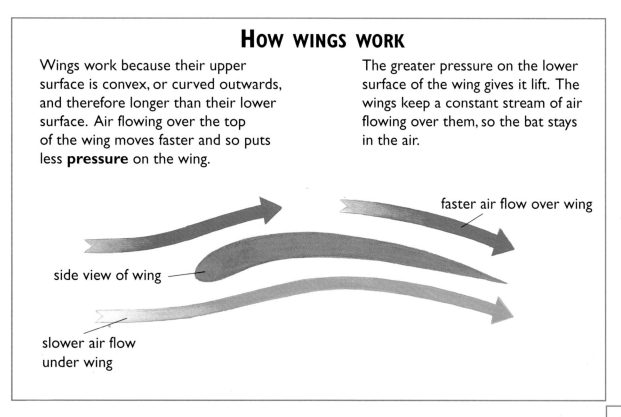

faster air flow over wing

side view of wing

slower air flow under wing

MAKING REPAIRS

Unlike the feathers of a bird's wing, the wing **membrane** of a bat is living tissue. A small hole in its wing heals completely in about 28 days, but a larger hole or tear does not heal. Unless the damage is very great, the bat can still fly.

RUNNING

Bats are so used to flying that being able to run on all fours is not an important means of movement. However, they are able to scurry around using their legs and wings.

Vampire bats can run and jump using their back legs and wrists with great agility. This is essential so that they can quickly hop out of harm's way, if necessary.

A bat has the same kinds of bones in its wings as you have in your arms, wrists and hands. The clawed thumb is used for gripping.

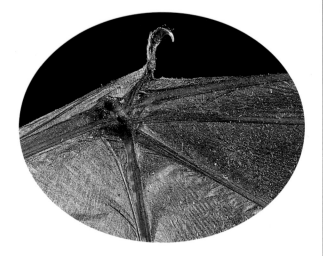

Bats 'run' on their wrists and ankles. Most are **agile** climbers, using their sharply clawed feet and the clawed thumb on their wings to grip.

A megabat wraps its wings closely around its body when it is resting in its tree roost.

It is much easier for a bat to take off from a hanging position than from the ground. A few bats do spend more time on the ground than others. Mouse-eared bats, free-tailed bats and vampire bats are the best runners.

RESTING

When resting, bats hang upside down, clinging to their **roost** with their feet. They do not fall, even when sleeping or **hibernating**, because their weight triggers a locking system that makes sure their clawed toes keep their grip.

Some bats cling to the sides of their roost when resting; others, such as horseshoe bats and many types of megabats, hang freely. When these bats are sleeping, they wrap their wings around themselves.

A greater horseshoe bat hangs upside down from a cave ceiling, gripping tightly with its toes. The bat's feet will continue to rest in this position even when the bat is asleep or hibernating.

Bat senses

Like other **mammals**, bats can see, hear, smell and touch, but they also use **echolocation** to **navigate**. Exactly how they manage to fly so fast at night without crashing into anything was a complete mystery until the first **ultrasound** microphone was invented in 1938. It was then that scientists began to understand how bats echolocate.

HOW ECHOLOCATION WORKS

A bat sends out bursts, or pulses, of high-pitched sound as it flies along. These sounds travel as sound waves through the air until

Bats use high-frequency sounds to find prey because these sounds have very short wavelengths, which are good for tracking down small objects and creatures such as insects (see diagram).

Using echolocation, it is possible for a bat to track down an object that is less than 1 millimetre wide.

Bats give off sound in very short pulses so that each pulse is completed before the echo bounces back.

When a bat gets really close to an insect, it may give off pulses of sound that last only a fraction of a millisecond.

HOW BATS ECHOLOCATE

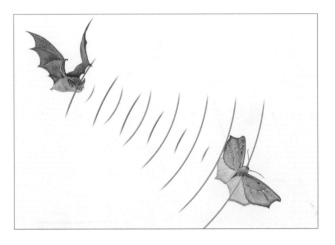

1. The pulses of sound made by a hunting bat hit a moth flying some distance away. The bat can tell exactly where the insect is, and how large it is, from the returning echo.

Bats like this greater horseshoe bat need to use echolocation to find their prey in the dark.

they hit an object. When this happens, some of the energy in the sound wave is absorbed by the object, but the rest bounces back, like a ball does if you throw it against a wall. The kind of echo that bounces back depends on how far away the object is, whether it is hard or soft, and whether it is moving or still. The bat is able to tell from these echoes what kind of object it is. As the sound waves travel through the air, they spread out in the shape of a cone. Each different **species** of bat has its own pattern of echolocation.

2. The bat flies towards the **prey**, using more pulses of **high-frequency** sound to track it down. As the bat gets closer, it makes faster and faster calls.

3. At last, the bat is almost close enough to its prey to catch it. At the point of contact, the calls made by the hungry bat are so fast that they are known as a 'feeding buzz'.

HIGH-FREQUENCY SOUNDS

Microbats make the sounds that they use in **echolocation** with their larynx (voice box). The rousette megabat makes clicks with its tongue to echolocate. Most bats send these sounds through the mouth. Others, such as horseshoe bats, send sound through the nose. These bats have complicated structures called noseleaves around their nostrils that help focus the beam of sound as it leaves.

Almost all of the sounds a bat makes when echolocating are too high for human adults to hear, although children can hear some of them. This is because these sounds are produced at a **high frequency** of over 20,000 cycles per second (20 kilo**hertz**). Most bats echolocate between 20–80kHz.

WHISPERS OR SHOUTS

Bats do not all echolocate at the same intensity, or loudness. It depends on the kind of environment they live in and the kind of **prey** they feed on. Loud sounds travel further than soft ones. Noctule bats, which live in Europe and **temperate** Asia, hunt in open spaces, and so have loud voices that can reach distant objects. Long-eared bats have quiet

NOSE ADAPTATIONS

Biologists are not sure exactly how the strangely shaped noses of some kinds of bats work. It is thought that the sometimes complicated arrangements of slits and flaps of skin help focus the sounds made by the bats into a narrow beam.

leaf-nosed bat

slit-faced bat

horseshoe bat

With its mouth wide open, this pipistrelle bat is sending the pulses of sound that will allow it to follow and catch this caddis fly.

voices, because they hunt among foliage and their voices do not need to carry as far.

FINDING PREY

A bat uses echolocation to find its favourite prey. When a bat locates a flying insect, it speeds up the rate at which it sends out sound, so that it can get a more exact picture of where the insect is, even in the darkness. This short and powerful burst of sound is called a 'feeding buzz'.

EYESIGHT

The saying 'as blind as a bat' is a strange one. Even the small eyes of most microbats can see well. Whenever there is enough light, bats are able to use their eyes to see with. Microbats that leave their **roosts** before it is fully dark use

On bright, moonlit nights, the California leaf-nosed bat uses its eyes as well as its ears to find and catch prey.

sight as well as **echolocation**. Megabats have excellent eyesight and are able to see well even in very little light.

Bat detectors

Small electronic instruments called 'bat detectors' are the best way to listen to bats as they fly about at night. Bat detectors turn the sounds that they make while echolocating into sounds that humans can hear. Because each species makes a different sound, bat detectors allow humans to **identify** many kinds as they fly past. Bats that make the loudest calls are the easiest to identify.

HEARING

All bats have noticeable ears and excellent hearing, but those that use echolocation have especially sensitive hearing. Because the pulses of sound made by some bats are very loud, echolocating bats become deaf for an instant while they are sending out sound. This is done by a movement of one of the tiny bones of the inner ear, and it keeps the bat from damaging its own sensitive ears.

Although they can echolocate, **species** such as the pallid bat of North and Central America, and the brown long-eared bat of Europe and **temperate** Asia, hunt by listening for the sounds that their **prey** makes. These 'listening' bats have huge ears so that they can pick up even the quietest sounds made by moths and other insects.

The ears of a brown long-eared bat are almost as long as its body. These amazing ears are sensitive enough to hear the flapping of a moth's wings.

Food and feeding

The diet of megabats is made up almost entirely of plants. Most kinds eat the fruits of **tropical** trees, which is why they are also known as fruit bats. Some eat flowers, nectar and pollen, and a few eat seeds.

Microbats eat a much wider range of food than megabats. Although most **species** eat insects or other **arthropods** such as scorpions, spiders and centipedes, the rest eat small **vertebrates**, including fish, frogs, small rats and even other bats. Others feed on fruit, flowers, or nectar. Vampire bats eat only blood (see page 27).

Eucalyptus flowers are the most important source of food for the grey-headed fruit bat from Australia, but it will eat fruit too.

Fruit bats help the trees on which they feed to reproduce by pollinating their flowers and by spreading their seeds.

The American long-nosed bat feeds mainly on nectar, which makes up as much as 75 per cent of its diet.

Some moths can hear the echolocation signals made by bats. When they do, they instantly fall to the ground to avoid being caught and eaten.

The Mexican long-nosed bat is only 80 millimetres long, but its tongue is almost the same length as its body.

A colony of Mexican free-tailed bats that is made up of more than 100,000 bats can eat at least 200 tonnes of insects in a year.

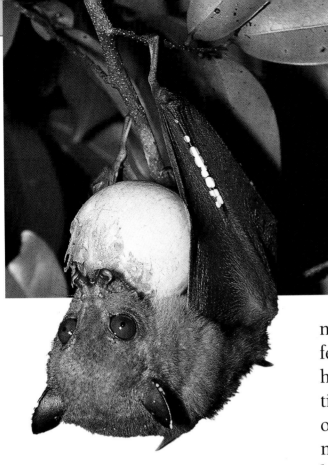

The Queensland tube-nosed bat feeds entirely on fruits, such as figs, which grow in the Australian rainforest.

Although there are no megabats in the tropical regions of North and South America, there are fruit-eating spear-nosed bats such as the Mexican fruit bat. Some spear-nosed bats, known as flower bats, feed on nectar from flowers. They have extremely long tongues, the tip of which has a sponge-like layer of fine hairs that soak up the liquid nectar. While they are feeding, these bats also **pollinate** the flowers.

EATING FRUIT

Fruit is heavy and often full of large seeds. A bat cannot fly as well when it is weighed down by a large meal, so it hangs while eating. The fruit is crushed to a pulp (mush) against the roof of the bat's mouth, then the juice and fruit is swallowed. It spits out the seeds and skin. Below a fruit-eating bat's feeding **roost**, there is a compost heap of seeds and droppings.

Blossom bats are 'flying foxes' with long tongues that have brush-like tips. These can reach right to the base of tubular flowers to mop up the sugary nectar.

INSECT EATERS

Bats eat truly enormous numbers of insects. Scientists have estimated that a bat may eat as much as half its own body weight of insects in a night. Different **species** often specialize in catching and eating different kinds of insects. Smaller bats, such as pipistrelles, eat tiny insects, including gnats. They have sharp

Pipistrelle bats are small – only about 40 millimetres long. Their sharp, tiny teeth are only able to crush up insects such as gnats, mosquitoes and small moths.

teeth, but these teeth are too small to allow them to feed on larger, tougher **prey**. Bigger bats, such as serotines from Europe, Asia and Africa, have stronger teeth, which allow them to eat beetles, crickets and cockroaches.

HUNTING

Insect-eating bats hunt their prey in different ways. The leaf-nosed bat attacks its prey from a perch. Each leaf-nosed bat has a number of perches in its territory. It scans its surroundings using **echolocation**, darting out to catch any insect that flies into its path. Fast-flying sheath-tailed bats and noctules catch insects flying in open spaces. Some bats, like Bechstein's bat from Europe and Iran, 'collect' insects and spiders by picking them off the leaves of trees. Others, such as the pallid bat, fly low over the ground, snatching up insects and other **invertebrates**.

Bats mostly catch their prey in their mouth, often using a swift flick of a wing tip or tail.

Small insects may be eaten in flight, but some kinds of bats carry larger prey to a feeding perch. These are easy to **identify** from the large pile of wings and other insect parts left on the ground below.

Serotine bats are much larger than pipistrelles – on average about 70 millimetres long. Their teeth are larger and their jaws more powerful, so they can eat large moths and even stag beetles.

25

CARNIVORES

At least six **species** of bat catch and eat animals such as small rats, mice, birds, frogs, lizards and even other bats. These **carnivorous** bats include the false vampires from India, Australian false vampires, or ghost bats, and American false vampires. They are large, powerful bats that are thought to snatch most of their **prey** either from the ground or from trees.

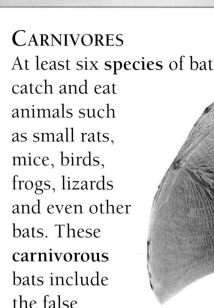

This Indian false vampire bat has no trouble at all carrying the mouse that it has caught to a quiet **roost**, to eat it.

The fringe-lipped bat of Central and South America eats mostly frogs. This bat lives in the rainforests of **tropical** America. It finds many of the frogs it eats by listening for the mating song of the male frog and then swooping down on its prey.

A fisherman bat skims slowly over the surface of rivers or lakes, using **echolocation** to find small ripples on the water that may mean a fish is near the surface. This bat has large feet with big claws to hook fish out of the water.

Vampires

There are three species of vampire bat, but only one of them feeds on the blood of **mammals**. The other two feed on bird blood. All three species live in tropical and **subtropical** regions of the Americas. The common vampire from Central and South America attacks wild and domestic animals. It lands near its sleeping prey and runs silently towards it. With razor-sharp front teeth, it slices away a piece of skin from a thin spot such as an ankle or ear. As the blood trickles out, the bat laps it up. The sleeping prey rarely wake up while this is happening, but the health of livestock, for example, can suffer from the loss of blood. Vampires can also pass on the deadly disease, rabies.

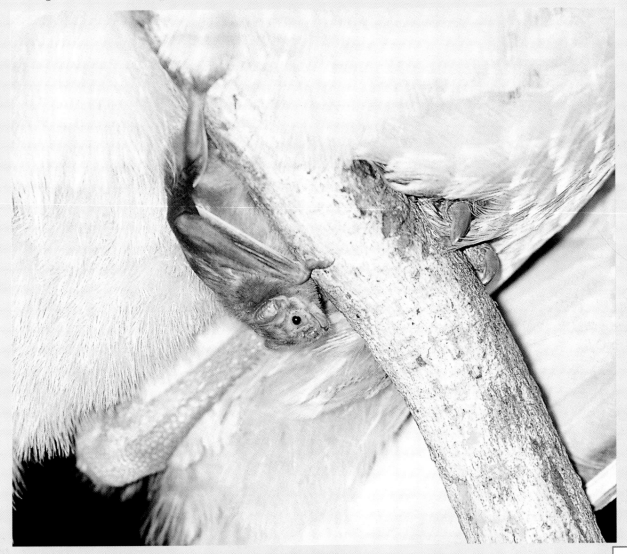

Bat roosts

Bats often live together in **colonies** for at least part of the year. At night, as long as the weather is not too cold, bats go out to search for food. By day, they need somewhere safe to rest. Male and female bats need somewhere to mate, and the females need somewhere to give birth and look after their young until they can fly. Some bats also need a place to **hibernate**.

Egyptian fruit bats roost and mate in caves or large, empty buildings. Each camp may have as many as 200–500 bats.

Some colonies of bats may have just a few members, but others are made up of hundreds, thousands or even millions of bats.

The red bat of North America is so tough it does not look for a special place to hibernate in winter – it just hangs from the branches of a tree.

The disc-winged bat of Central and tropical South America has suction pads at the base of its thumbs and on its feet so it can cling to the smooth surface of the rolled leaves in which it roosts.

The leaf-nosed bat, which roosts on tree-trunks, has fur that is patterned to look just like the bark on which it rests.

ROOSTS

All of the different places that bats use when they are not flying around are called **roosts**. Different **species** roost in different places. Bats rarely use the same roost for all their activities, but they may return to the same set of roosts every year. Many megabats simply roost in a tree, in a large group called a '**camp**'.

TREE ROOSTS

In warm regions, some bats simply roost by clinging to tree trunks or among leafy vines, but those that live in **temperate** parts of the world need more shelter. The noctule of Europe and Asia, and the North

Large, hollow trunks are used as roosts year-round by bats such as this noctule bat.

American evening bat roost in holes in trees. Barbastelles, the Indiana myotis and others often roost under loose bark.

Many megabats, like these little red flying foxes, roost simply by hanging from the branches of a tree.

A lesser horseshoe bat wraps up well against the cold while hibernating in an old mine in Wales.

This way they are able to save energy until the weather warms up.

HIBERNATION ROOSTS

In winter, bats need a cool place to **roost** where they can lower their body temperature and so save energy, but not so cold that they freeze to death. The place of hibernation also needs to be humid, because bats lose moisture through their furless wings. Bats hibernate in all sorts of places – in hollow trees, caves or holes between the stonework of buildings.

HIBERNATION

In some parts of the world, the insects that many bats feed on are hard to find during cold winters. To survive these periods, bats **hibernate**. They enter a deep, sleep-like state in which their breathing slows and their body temperature falls.

Near Nietoperek, Poland, as many as 30,000 bats of 12 different species hibernate every year in a maze of underground tunnels built during World War II.

Tent-making bats

About 18 **species** of **tropical** bat make their own roosts from large leaves. The white bat from Central America uses banana or *Heliconia* leaves to make its roost. The white bat lives in small groups of up to six. The bats bite through the tough side veins along each side of the leaf, so that the two sides of the leaf drop down to make a tent over them.

I DIDN'T KNOW THAT

CAVES

Caves are ideal places for many kinds of bats to roost. They are fairly safe from most **predators**. The inside of a cave is often damp and has a range of temperatures so the bats can go deeper or stay near the entrance, depending on their needs, or the outside temperature. In the tropics and **subtropics**, bats roost in caves all year round.

MIGRATION

If they cannot find anywhere to hibernate in winter, bats may have to **migrate**. In winter, some hoary bats fly as far as 1700 kilometres (1050 miles), all the way from Canada to California, Texas and South Carolina, USA. The warmer weather there means they have plenty of insects to eat, so they do not have to hibernate at all.

Reproduction

Much about the lives of many kinds of bats remains unknown, including how they choose mates. Most kinds of bats do not form pairs. Instead, male bats try to attract a number of females, and both males and females may mate with more than one partner.

Some male bats, for example male noctules, attract females by calling from their **roosts**. Some, such as male pipistrelles, let females know where they are by using a special song flight. Each male flies around his mating roost making an **ultrasound** 'song' that is quite different from the calls they make when hunting for **prey**. Others, such as male fisherman bats, have scent **glands** that

A male crested free-tailed bat from Africa has a crest of stiff hairs that it raises to impress female bats.

The lesser white-lined bat from tropical America is one of just a few bats that stays together with its mate in a pair. They often roost with other pairs.

A male spear-nosed bat mates with a group of up to 25 females for many years.

Female North American red bats usually give birth to two or three young at a time, and sometimes as many as five.

The hammer-headed bat from Africa has the noisiest courtship of the bat world. The males have a large, hammer-like muzzle with a huge voice box and nasal passages. This enables them to make loud noises, which can be clearly heard by people.

At about three weeks old, this young pipistrelle is nearly full-grown and ready to fly. However, it still needs its mother's milk for food.

produce musky smells to attract a mate. Male bats are not known to help in any way with bringing up their young.

In **temperate** parts of the world, microbats mate in the autumn, although mating happens from time to time throughout winter as well. Females of many kinds of bat do not get pregnant at this time. Instead, they store the male sex cells until spring, when they come out of **hibernation**. Bats are usually born in early summer, which gives the young enough time to fatten up on insects before the weather gets cold and food is in short supply.

Most female bats give birth to a single young, just once a year. A few bats do have twins, and some of those in **tropical** regions may give birth more than once a year. Like other **mammals**, young bats feed on their mother's milk.

Newborn microbats have no fur to keep them warm, which is why it is important for the females to choose somewhere warm to give birth.

THE NURSERY COLONY

Even in spring or summer, the weather can be chilly in **temperate** regions. Bats may greatly slow down their **metabolism** in this case, but a pregnant female tries to avoid doing so. This is because if her temperature falls, her baby will develop more slowly.

To keep warm, female bats may **roost** together in a nursery **colony**. When it is time to give birth, a female bat turns the other way up and hangs from her thumbs, using her tail flap and wings to stop the tiny young bat from falling.

When a megabat is born, its eyes are open and it is covered with fur. A newborn microbat has no fur, and its eyes are closed. Most bats are born with milk teeth, which are hooked for extra grip onto their mother's fur and **teats**. Very young bats, often called pups, need constant warmth so that they can grow quickly. They cannot control their temperature very well, so the

Nursery colonies of common bent-winged bats may have many thousands of females and their young. Amazingly, returning mothers are able to pick out their own pups.

females keep their young huddled together in a warm roost in a nursery colony. This means that the tiny bats do not get cold when their mothers fly off.

GROWING UP

Although a female bat can carry her pup around while it is still small, sometimes carrying it to different roosts, she usually leaves it behind while she goes out to feed. When she returns, mother and pup find and recognize each other by sound and smell. In as little as two to three weeks, the young bats are ready to fly. It takes longer for them to learn to find food for themselves, and they continue to feed on their mother's milk for a few more weeks. When the young can fend for themselves, the nursery colony breaks up.

STAYING ALIVE

For their size, bats are amazingly long-living **mammals**. However,

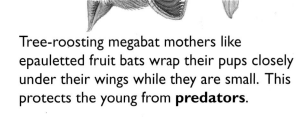

Tree-roosting megabat mothers like epauletted fruit bats wrap their pups closely under their wings while they are small. This protects the young from **predators**.

the first year is a dangerous time for a young bat and many die during this period, especially if they cannot find enough food to ensure survival over winter. Survivors have a good chance of living 7 to 8 years, and there are records of bats living for 30 years or more in the wild.

Enemies and threats

The bat populations in many parts of the world are falling. Bats have many natural enemies, but the main reason for this fall in numbers is **habitat** destruction caused by humans. Bats need somewhere to **roost** by day, a safe place to give birth, somewhere to search for food and, in many regions of the world, somewhere to **hibernate**. If any of these habitats are destroyed, life becomes difficult for the bats that have depended on them. Because bats reproduce so slowly, the population in an area takes a long time to recover if there is a major fall in numbers.

By day, long-nosed bats roost out in the open on tree trunks or lichen-covered rocks by streams in **tropical** rainforests. Their colour and pattern help to hide them from enemies.

Twelve species of bat may have become extinct in the last half of the 20th century.

All but 3 of the 30 known species of bat in Europe are classed as endangered, rare or vulnerable.

Fruit bat 'camps' of an estimated 30 million bats were recorded in Australia in the 1930s. Today, only a few of these camps are thought to contain more than 100,000 fruit bats.

On tropical islands such as Fiji and Samoa, typhoons sometimes destroy colonies of fruit bats.

The large fruit bat is at risk in Malaysia and Indonesia because the mangrove forests in which it roosts are being cut down for timber.

The brown tree snake has badly affected the numbers of Marianas fruit bats as well as many species of birds living on the island of Guam.

NATURAL ENEMIES

Although they can fly, bats are still **prey** for a number of **predators**. These include snakes, birds of prey, monkeys, racoons, large spiders and cats. The false vampires of India and Australia even eat other bats.

Domestic cats are probably the biggest 'natural' enemy of bats that live near human populations. Cats often wait for bats as they leave their roosts under low roofs.

The bat hawk of Borneo catches bats at dusk, when they leave their roosts, and again at dawn, when they return. The bat hawk swallows the bats whole, so it can catch and eat as many as possible while it hunts.

The Marianas fruit bat on the island of Guam, in the Pacific, is at great risk from the brown tree snake. The snake is not from the island, but was introduced there in the late 1940s. Brown tree snakes are expert climbers and catch large numbers of baby bats before they can fly. The snake is now the greatest threat to this **species** of bat on Guam.

HUMAN THREATS

Fruit bats are a source of food for many people. On Guam, humans have eaten bats for more than 1000 years. By the 1960s, fruit bats became so rare that people began importing them from neighbouring islands. One **species**, Tokuda's fruit bat, has already died out.

CHEMICALS AND INSECTICIDES

When people build houses and other buildings, they increase the number of places in which bats can **roost**. Because most bats are **nocturnal**, people often do not know they are there. When people treat these buildings with chemicals to kill insects, bats that live there can be harmed.

The increased use of **insecticides** and other chemicals in farming has

Killing insects and other pests with chemical sprays helps crops grow well, but also reduces the amount of insects available for bats and birds to eat.

also added to the serious fall of many bat populations. Insecticides reduce the numbers of insects that bats can feed on. Bats cannot get enough to eat before winter arrives, and many do not survive until spring. When they eat insects affected by chemicals, those chemicals affect the bats' health.

People sometimes deliberately kill bats, either because they are frightened of them or because they believe bats spread disease. Fruit bats are sometimes killed because they eat fruit grown to be sold. Roosting grey-headed fruit bats are sometimes shot because they feed on these kind of fruit trees.

Mexican free-tailed bats

In 1964, 25 million Mexican free-tailed bats lived in a **colony** in Eagle Creek Cave, Arizona, USA. The use of insecticides to control insect pests poisoned many bats and reduced their food supply. By the 1970s, there were only an estimated 600,000 left in Eagle Creek Cave. A reduction in the use of such chemicals has allowed numbers to rise, but not to their former levels.

I DIDN'T KNOW THAT

Conservation

Because of the many threats to bat populations around the world, it is now clear that a worldwide programme of protection is needed. The populations of many **species**, whether they live in cities, towns, villages or in natural environments, such as forests, are falling. Bats are an important part of our environment and the way it works. They control insect populations, which is important both to human health and

Old mines and caves are often important for hibernating bats, but they can be dangerous places for people. To protect such places, and to stop people from hurting themselves, the entrances are made safe with bat grilles that stop people from wandering in, but let bats fly in and out.

Putting nets around orchards is one way of keeping fruit bats away from the fruit without harming them, but it is expensive.

British biologists have recently discovered that the common pipistrelle is actually two different species of pipistrelle.

Wood used in buildings is often treated with chemicals to stop it being attacked by insect pests. Some of these chemicals used in the past also killed bats, but today, safer, more bat-friendly chemicals are used.

farming. They also **pollinate** many **tropical** fruit trees and help spread their seeds.

BAT CONSERVATION ORGANIZATIONS

Planning international efforts for bat conservation is the work of organizations such as the **Chiroptera** Specialist Group of the World Conservation Union's Species Survival Commission.

In the UK, the Bat Conservation Trust (BCT) is a charity that helps bat conservation. The BCT runs the National Bat Monitoring Programme – a scheme that uses volunteers all over the country to find out about the populations of rare species of bats. Each volunteer counts how many of these bats he or she hears on a bat detector in a particular area. Results are sent to the BCT, which can keep track if numbers of bats are falling or increasing.

Most counties in the UK also have their own Bat Group. Each group carries out practical bat conservation work as well as organizing interesting activities and talks about bats. They are fun for all the family!

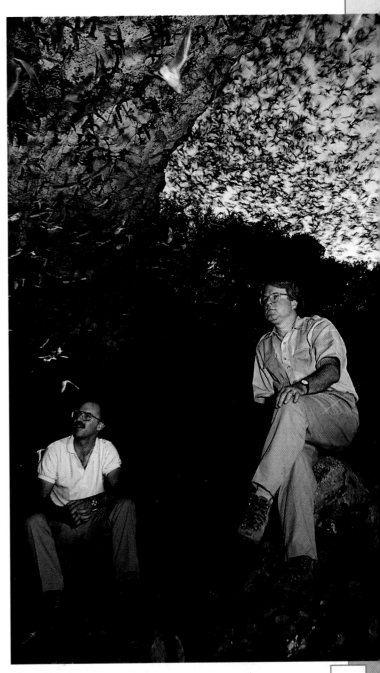

There is still very little known about many bat species. In order to draw up plans to help bats, bat conservationists spend a lot of their time studying them, including their **roosts** and foraging areas.

HELPING BATS

There is a lot that people can do to help bats. Bat boxes can be put up on trees that are too young to have holes or splits in them, giving bats a place to **roost**. Caves or old mine shafts can be gated, or grilled, making them safe for **hibernating** bats and at the same time reducing the danger to people. Artificial roosts can also be built.

STUDYING BATS

There is still much for humans to learn, about even the most common **species** of bats. Because bats are **nocturnal**, finding out exactly where they go to feed and roost is difficult. Locating tree roosts is especially difficult. Scientists sometimes clip a band or ring around a bone in a bat's wing. This allows them to study specific bat populations to find out, for example, if they return to the same place to hibernate each year and how long they live. Scientists also use radio-tracking devices to help in their study of bat populations.

The trees in many forests are too young to have 'nooks' for bat roosts. Bat boxes provide somewhere for woodland bats to roost. With regular inspections, conservationists can check how this helps local bats.

Rodrigues fruit bats

The Rodrigues fruit bat was once common on the small island of Rodrigues, which is about 560 kilometres (900 miles) west of the island of Mauritius in the Indian Ocean. On Rodrigues, the clearing of tamarind forests, a food source and **habitat**, together with cyclone destruction and hunting by humans, resulted in a serious fall in the population in the last half of the 20th century. Wildlife laws now protect the Rodrigues fruit bat. A captive breeding programme in nine zoos in Mauritius, the UK and USA has been so successful that there are plans to introduce captive-bred bats into the wild.

Glossary

agile quick-moving

air resistance force that affects an object as it moves through the air. Air resistance pushes against the moving object and slows it down.

arthropod invertebrate animal that has a tough outer layer called a cuticle, or exoskeleton

camp large group of roosting megabats

carnivore animal that eats mainly other animals

Chiroptera order, or group, of mammals that we know as bats

colony large number of animals of the same species, living closely together

cusp pointed tip of a tooth

echolocation way in which a bat uses sound to navigate and find food in the dark. The bat sends out a burst, or pulse, of sounds and then listens to the echoes that bounce back. The echoes tell the bat what and where objects are.

endotherm animal such as a mammal or bird that can control its own constant body temperature

gland organ in an animal's body that produces specific substances

habitat natural home of an animal or plant

hertz unit that measures sound frequency (how high or low a sound is). A kilohertz is 1000 Hertz.

hibernation deep, sleep-like state in which some animals spend the cold months of winter

high frequency sounds too high for people to hear

identify to recognize or know what something is

humid moist or damp

insecticide substance used for killing insects

invertebrate animal that does not have a backbone, such as an insect, centipede or spider

limbs legs, arms or wings

mammal animal with hair or fur, whose young feed on milk produced by their mother

membrane thin, sheet-like layer

metabolism all the chemical changes that occur in an animal or plant, for example those involved in digesting food and turning it into energy

migration seasonal movement of animals from one area to another

navigate steer or guide

nocturnal animal that sleeps during the day and is active at night

pollination transfer of male pollen to female flower parts to produce seed

predator animal that hunts another animal for food

pressure pressing force

prey animal that is caught and eaten by another animal for food

roost place used by a bat when it is not flying around

species kind, or type, of living thing

subtropical coming from parts of the world that are hot, but not as hot as the tropics

teats parts of a mammal through which mik is sucked by its young

temperate mild temperatures, neither extremely hot nor extremely cold

tropical coming from or to do with the extremely hot parts of the world known as the tropics

ultrasound sounds that are too high for humans to hear

vertebrate animal that has a backbone

wingspan distance from one wingtip to the other, when the wings are stretched out

Further information

Books

Animals in Order: Bats: Mammals That Fly, Marlene Sway (Franklin Watts, 1999)

Bats, Lily Wood (Scholastic, 2001)

Bats of the British Isles, Tony Wardaugh (Shire Publications Ltd, 1995)

Eyewitness Juniors: Amazing Bats, Frank Greenaway (Random House Children's Publishing, 1991)

Young Explorers Series: Vampire Bats, Kimberly Williams and Erik Stoops (Faulkner's Publishing Group, 2000)

Websites

The website for Bat Conservation International: www.batcon.org

The website for The Bat Conservation Trust: www.bats.org.uk

Disclaimer
All the Internet addresses (URLs) given in this book were valid at the time of going to press. However, due to the dynamic nature of the Internet, some addresses may have changed, or sites may have ceased to exist since publication. While the author and publishers regret any inconvenience this may cause readers, no responsibility for any such changes can be accepted by either the author or the publishers.

Index

Numbers in *italic* indicate pictures

large fruit bat 36
leaf-nosed bat 13, *18*, 25, 28
    California leaf-nosed bat *20*
lesser white-lined bat 32
lifespan 35
little brown bat 9, 12
little red flying fox *29*
long-eared bat 18
    brown long-eared bat 21, *21*
long-nosed bat 22, *36*
    Mexican long-nosed bat 22
long-tongued bat 12

mammals 6, 33, 35
Marianas fruit bat 37
mating 12, 28, 32–33
megabats 6, 8, 15, *15*, 18, 20, 22–23, 28,
    34–35
microbats 6, 7, 9, 18, 20, 22, 33, 34
migration 9, 31
mines 40–42, *40*
mouse-eared bat 15
moustached bat 13
Myotis chiloensis 9

National Bat Monitoring Programme 41
noctule bat 9, 18, 25, 29, *29*, 32
noses 11, 18, *18*
nursery colonies 34–35, *34*
nursing young 6, 33–35

painted bat 10
pallid bat 21, 25
pipistrelle *19*, 24, *24*, 32–33, *32–33*, 40
pollination 23, 41
predators 31, 37

Queensland tube-nosed bat *23*

rabies 27
red bat 10, 28, 32

reproduction 32–35, 36
resting 7–8, 15, *15*, 28
Rodrigues fruit bat 43, *43*
roosting 12, 15, 23, 28–31, 35, 42
rousette megabat 18
running 14–15

serotine bat 24, *25*
short-tailed bat 12, *12*
sleeping 12, 15
slit-faced bat 11, *18*
spear-faced bat *11*
spear-nosed bat 23, 32
spotted bat 10
subtropics 8, 27, 31

tails 7–9, 12
teeth 7–9, *9*, 24, *24*, *25*, 34
thumbs 7, 14, *14*, 28
Tokuda's fruit bat 38
tropics 6, 8, 10, 27, 31

ultrasound 16, 32

vampire bats *14*, 15, 22, 27
    common vampire bat 27

white bat 31, *31*
wings 6–7, 12–15, 30
World Conservation Union 41
wrinkle-faced bat 11